Abby J's
FarmStyle Living
COOKBOOK

By Abby Jackson

Abby J's
FarmStyle Living
COOKBOOK

By Abby Jackson ~ Abby J's Gourmet

Designed and Published by Nancy Suttles
Suttles Design, LLC

Printed in the United States of America

ISBN: 978-0-692--44443-65295

ACKNOWLEDGMENTS

A heartfelt thank you to my wonderful family and friends, especially to my husband, John Jackson, who has shared his love and support all these years. He has been my number one fan and taste tester. He has also given me a life that allows me to pursue my passion for food and a love to share it with others.

To my Blackhawk family, which includes so many wonderful people—if you are reading this you know who you are and how you have made a difference in my life and how these memories will last a lifetime.

Special thanks to Juanita Walls, who always gave me encouragement and mentored me during my early years while living in Savannah, Georgia.

I am also thankful for my good friends who have made my farmstyle cooking classes a success—we have had a lot of fun, and I have learned alot from each of you. More good times are coming!

A special thanks to Nancy Suttles, my publisher, for putting up with me. Your influence in my life is immeasurable, and I appreciate your creativity, dedication and hard work.

My biggest thanks are to my parents. My father worked very hard making sure I had all the things I needed including a good education. My mother has always been my canning partner, showing me how it's done. Thank you for all the food that you have put on the table. You have always gone the extra mile taking care of others, and you make the very best of every situation. Your godly influence will always be with me.

Forward

By Dan Quarles

Almost two years following the beginning of the 21st century, on a crisp September day, I was out in the back of our condo in Signal Mountain, Tennessee minding my own business. The new neighbor across the way was in the process of moving in. He yelled "you a fly fisherman?" I replied, "sort of, when I have time." He said we should go fishing sometime. I agreed. He then asked, "Have you ever fished Blackhawk?" I replied, I had not, "What is it?" I asked. He said "Blackhawk and trophy trout fishing are . . . just unforgettable." He continued: "It is a picturesque, pristine trout river in the north Georgia mountains, just north of Clarkesville, Georgia.

Three weeks later, my neighbor, his son and I struck out to visit Blackhawk. Upon arrival, we met our guide, and then through the door of the farmhouse emerged the lady that I would grow to cherish, "love" and greatly respect. Mrs. John Jackson, better known as Abby J. She was all business in a Southern sort of way. She shook our hands and announced: "Lunch is at 12:30 on the dot; your guide will take good care of you, now go get 'em!" After a few hours, I caught the biggest rainbow trout I had ever seen. The rest is history.

Over the years, I have averaged between two and four trips a year to Blackhawk. Upon arrival, I may get a hug or a hip bump or a "peck on the cheek." Our lunches are always, delicious, hearty and pleasantly presented. Homemade soup is to die for; I am partial to Abby J's signature chili on crisp fall days and really cold spring days. Usually there are fresh baked breads, delicious desserts and other tempting goodies. The food at Blackhawk is always great.

In college I was a chemistry major. I always said if you could read you could be a chemist or a cook. That may be true, however, Abby J is more than a cook, she is so much more. She is a chef—a student of the culinary arts and a darn good teacher of the art of preparing a feast. I've been known to be a meat and three kind of person. When Abby creates her magic in the kitchen, I get my meat and three— or four or more —plus a soup, appetizers, fresh bread, juices, fruit, drinks and desserts, all packaged in an eye and palate pleasing presentation.

In the early days, I felt like Abby was using our lunches as trial balloons. Honing her craft, you might say. Even the sandwiches, garnished with special herbs, sauces and seasonings were and still are delicious. One of the first times I saw Abby in the kitchen was at one of her cooking schools. My wife and I attended, and we were mesmerized. What a sensory delight. I'll never forget the time I called to make a reservation to fish, and was informed, "Oh, she's in Italy at a cooking school." Then she traveled to France, the wine country and other destinations too numerous to detail. She is still honing her craft. I remember some years ago about a show called the "Galloping Gourmet." If the title fits, wear it, Abby J.

This is not just any cookbook. This is Abby J's travelogue of sorts. It is a reflection of her quest for the best in the culinary arts. It reflects her journey as she continues to expand her culinary knowledge.

Abby is too modest to admit it, but she is "REALLY GOOD AT WHAT SHE DOES." I know you, the reader, will enjoy this cookbook as much as she has enjoyed making the trip. So as she said the first time I met her, I say "go get 'em, and enjoy!!!"

Photo > Wade Collins

Welcome!

Smokin' hot and full of flavor is what I would like to share with you in this cookbook.

I hope these recipes will entice you to come back for more, time and time again!

As a farmer's daughter growing up with five brothers, I learned how to live in a man's world. There was never a dull moment. My grandmother taught me all she could by giving me chores to do and making every minute count. I can't begin to tell you how many times we found her in the garden having an asthma attack, and thinking she was going to heaven. I remember the ambulance coming to get her, but her passion for being out in her garden, having her hands in the dirt, continued after many "attacks!"

There are some things in life that you never forget. One of the things my grandmother taught us was hard work, and another was the appreciation of the harvest. She taught us about true "farm-to-table," and sharing it with others. Growing up in the north Georgia mountains, you learn to appreciate good food and friends—a true Southern staple. I have so many great memories of cooking with my mother and grandmother, however, I know my passion comes from my grandmother. My family still has a working farm, where they enjoy that very same passion today.

Over the years my biggest pleasure has been cooking for my friends and going to places all over the world to expand my culinary knowledge. I have traveled to Italy and France and will attend a farm-to-table boot camp this summer at the Culinary Institute of America at Greystone in Napa Valley. I especially love Napa Valley—visiting the farms, wineries and cultivating new friends who share my same passion about supporting local farmers.

In 1996, my husband, John, and I opened Blackhawk Flyfishing on the Soque River. I've had the opportunity to cook for so many who have "wet a line" on our river and I continue to cook for my anglers, their families and others who I consider extended family. They have really enjoyed my dinners and cooking classes, which illustrate so much about my passion for fresh local food and celebrating harvest.

I believe in BIG flavor and using peppers, herbs and spices as a healthier way to prepare and flavor meals. I love to grow, explore and gather the freshest, local ingredients available. I believe that your dish can only be as good as what you begin with. Once you start eating healthy and buying local, you'll never want to stop cooking those fresh and healthy meals over and over again.

Each June, we open the Soque River Farmer's Market at our farm. We invite vendors from all over the region to participate. What I love the most is meeting folks and offering them the best in locally grown produce and handcrafted products. When you see all the smiles as people arrive, you know you're doing something that everyone has looked forward to.

As a Southerner at heart, you are what you eat, and it shows from the inside out. "Smokin' hot and full of flavor" is what I would like to share with you in this cookbook. I hope these recipes will entice you to come back for more. As my grandmother would say … let's all enjoy the fruits of our labor. Let's get cookin'!

Abby J

Creating this cookbook has been years in the making. The recipes I have included are all "tried and true," and most of all, they are favorites of so many. I hope you enjoy making them as much as I have, for my customers, friends and family.

Let's stay in touch!
abbyjsgourmet.com
abbyj@windstream.net

Contents

Fresh & Local

We have been growing fresh veggies and herbs for years on our farm. I was growing for Ford Fry's restaurants in Atlanta , No. 246, The Optmist and others, however this got so time consuming and overwhelming that I decided to open the Soque River Farmers Market here at Blackhawk and share the local harvest with everyone. We opened in June 2014 and we stay open on most Saturday's throughout the summer. My vision is to help entrepreneurs get started, and I invite anyone with a farm fresh product or service to come out and present on market day for free. This is my way of giving back and trying to support the local agriculture economy.

In 2011, I launched Abby J's Farm-to-Table Gourmet, a line of premium salsas and hot sauces—I started with two products and now I have five. Many of the recipes in this cookbook have my salsas and hot sauce in them and I have been asked over and over for these recipes—so I am now ready to share my " farm to table" style with everyone.

Smokin' Hot!

I add a little heat to almost everything!

I love fresh jalapeños, chili peppers and chili powder. Spicy foods help
remove toxins and also help increase metabolism to burn fat.
There is less need to salt everything when you can flavor with pepper,
and most importantly, it is much healthier for you!

~ Abby J ~

Herbs & Spices

I also love fresh ground pepper, cumin, garlic and basil. With this combination, you can enhance any dish. Fresh basil is a favorite because I enjoy making pesto every summer. The freshness that you can preserve for a winter's day is amazing.

I normally add fresh Parmesan cheese after I take my pesto out of the freezer to give it that extra kick of fresh FLAVOR! This is truly a favorite of so many that have had my gourmet sandwiches.

I enjoy homegrown summer flavor all year by drying herbs. Herb leaves should be cut when the plant's essential oils are at its highest. You can cut many herbs four times during the season. You should only cut herbs in the morning after the dew is off the plants. I like to gather my herbs in a bunch and tie them with the leafy ends down, so that the essential oils in the stems will flow into the leaves. I then hang them in my kitchen. I especially like using dried herbs in my recipes to add more flavor, especially to my chili recipe. There are other methods, however this is really the simplest of all and most economical.

Abby J's Special Rub

Ingredients:
2 teaspoons cayenne pepper
12 tablespoons brown sugar
8 tablespoons chili powder
8 tablespoons granulated garlic
7 tablespoons kosher salt
20 tablespoons paprika
8 tablespoons freshly ground pepper

Mix all the spices together. This rub can be used on pork, poultry, beef, chili and soups. Store up to 4 months in airtight container.

Canning & Preserving

One of my favorite times of the year is when my farm is overflowing with beautiful vine ripe tomatoes and bright green peppers. I enjoy preserving this bounty and savoring these summer memories to enjoy with my friends all throughout the year. There are many ways to preserve, but my favorite is to can most of my harvest, especially the tomatoes. I also make tons of pesto, which I use when preparing lunches for my clients. I freeze it in pint jars, and it keeps very well.

I love seeing the smiles on all those that are lucky to receive a jar of my jelly or my Christmas jalapeños. These homemade gifts are ones that folks never forget—and believe me—they will come back begging for more, especially if they can warm up a dish on a cold winter's night or use it to entertain and add some real flavor to a party. It goes without saying that you feel good about preserving and knowing exactly what is in every jar. I also find it to be economical, and it makes more sense to have the best in your pantry.

The pleasure I get from canning and preserving is overwhelming. It truly is a joy to share the harvesting, preparing and preserving not only with family but also with others, so they can appreciate the freshness of the season and also pass it on to others as I have done.

Remember, if you get a jar of my jalapeños, they will be from my farm to your table!

Farmstyle Living

ON THE SOQUE RIVER

FARM LIFE

*Most folks cannot connect to farm life because they don't live on a farm.
Some folks pretend to share in this bounty, but they do not get the day-to-day, on-the-job experience.
I have been blessed to come from a farming family. I truly love sharing these experiences,
such as canning, cooking and fishing on our farm, with others.
It truly is amazing… and my farm lifestyle is irreplaceable.*

FLY FISHING

*I love fly fishing. There is nothing more majestic than standing in the Soque River,
shaded by 100-year-old trees, to make you appreciate God's beauty.
This is more than just fishing; it is an experience that makes
the most indelible memories for me.*

FARMHOUSE

*We felt that we needed to live on the property to take better care of our clients,
so we decided to build our home on the river. When I was dating John, I fell in love with
a stone house in Blowing Rock, North Carolina. I never knew that I would be
building our dream home 10 years later, but we did it!
I am very thankful for my husband, John, and for him making my dreams come true.*

Roasting Peppers

There is nothing better than firing up the Big Green Egg and roasting fresh peppers
from my garden. I love baking, grilling, smoking, and roasting on my Big Green Egg.
There is something very satisfying about cooking with live fire.

My favorite peppers to roast are poblanos, jalapeños, and bell peppers.
To get that smoky, robust flavor the Big Green Egg is the key.

~ Cooking Tip ~
Place the peppers in a brown paper bag while hot and make sure to seal completely.
The steam that's trapped softens the skin and makes it easy to peel off.

Abby J's Salsas

I love Salsa because it is all about the FLAVOR.
Salsa is a hit for any party or social gathering it's especially a favorite of my fly fisherman and they always come back for more. Salsa is also a must on eggs and it's a great way to start your day!

Habanero Salsa
Serves 6-8

Ingredients
4 large tomatoes
2 habanero chiles
3 garlic cloves
1 small red onion
2 jalapeño diced
2 tablespoons lemon juice
½ teaspoon salt

Directions
Seed and dice the tomatoes and place them in a large bowl. Roast chiles cut them in half, scrape out the seeds and remove the seeds.

Finely chop the chiles ad add them to tomatoes. Dice the onion and garlic and add them to mixture. Sprinkle the lemon juice and salt over the top and fold the mixture to incorporate it. Let the salsa rest in the refrigerator overnight so the flavors can fully blend. Let the salsa return to room temperature before serving.

Jalapeño Mango Salsa
Serves 4-6

Ingredients
3 plum tomatoes
2 mangoes
2 jalapeños diced
½ red onion
1 garlic clove
¾ cup cilantro leaves
½ teaspoon of salt
½ teaspoon white pepper
1 tablespoon lemon juice
1 tablespoon olive oil

Directions
Chop the tomatoes and discard the seeds. Cut the mango in small chunks. Cut the stem off the jalapeño and remove the seeds; finely dice. Chop the onion, garlic and cilantro. Place all ingredients in a large bowl and toss until combined. Place the salsa in an airtight container and refrigerate overnight to allow the flavors to incorporate.

Photo > Wade Collins

Breakfast

Blueberry Lemon Muffins
Makes 8 muffins

Ingredients
1 ¼ cups all-purpose flour
1 egg
1 egg yolk
3 tablespoons freshly squeezed lemon juice
½ cup sugar
¼ cup sweet butter
½ teaspoon salt
½ teaspoon baking soda
1 teaspoon lemon zest
¾ cup fresh blueberries

Directions
Preheat oven to 350 degrees. In a mixing bowl, cream butter and sugar. Add lemon juice, egg and egg yolk. Mix well. In separate bowl combine flour, baking soda, salt, and lemon zest. Gently fold into butter mixture. Spoon batter into greased muffin pan. Arrange blueberries over top before baking. Bake for 15 minutes at 350 degrees.

Mountain Honey Cashew Butter
Makes 1 cup

Ingredients
1 cup unsalted roasted cashews
3 tablespoons of Oliver Sunflower Oil
2 teaspoons mountain honey, or more to taste
⅛ teaspoon fine salt

Directions
Combine the cashews, oil, honey and salt in a food processor. Process the nut mixture for 30 seconds. Scape down the side with a spatula, and then process to the desired smoothness. Add more sunflower oil, 1 teaspoon at a time, if a smoother butter is desired. Adjust the honey and salt to taste. Transfer to serving bowl and serve with cherry oat bread or crackers. This can be used in place of peanut butter and can be stored in airtight container for 2 months. To serve, allow it to come to room temperature for easier spreading.

Betty's Biscuits
Makes 1 dozen

Ingredients
2 cups self-rising flour
1 cup whipping cream

Directions
Preheat oven to 425 degrees. Combine ingredients and roll out—do not over handle dough. Bake for 10 to 12 minutes or until browned.

As they say, "early to bed, early to rise" especially when you have anglers eager to get on the Soque River going after the "monster." Early mornings are my favorite because I get to start my day with so much excitement with my three black labs—they are my Blackhawk greeters.

My anglers love it when I cook a farm fresh breakfast with farm fresh eggs, grits and some of my bean and jalapeño salsa. As most of my clients would say, "one bite, and you are hooked"… one way or another!

Mushroom, Hot Sausage and Jalapeño Quiche
Serves 6

Ingredients
1 deep-dish pie crust
8 ounces hot pork sausage
2 eggs
1 small carton baby portobello mushrooms, chopped
1 large jalapeño diced
¾ cup cup Swiss cheese, grated
¾ cup cheddar cheese, grated
½ cup milk
½ cup mayonnaise
1 tablespoon cornstarch

Directions
Preheat oven to 350 degrees. Cover edges of crust with foil and brown bottom of pie crust. In a large bowl, whisk together milk, eggs, mayonnaise and cornstarch until smooth. Add sausage, mushrooms, cheeses, pepper and combine thoroughly. Pour mixture into pie crust and bake 45 minutes or until golden.

Crepes
16 crepes

Ingredients
2 large eggs
¾ cup milk
½ cup water
1 cup flour
Butter (to coat the pan)

Directions
In a blender, combine all the ingredients and pulse for 10 seconds. Place the crepe batter in the refrigerator for 1 hour. This allows the bubbles to subside, so the crepes will be less likely to tear during cooking. The batter will keep up to 48 hours.

Heat a small non-stick pan. Add butter to coat. Pour 1 ounce of batter into the center of the pan; swirl and spread e[v]... 30 seconds and flip. Cook another 10 seconds and remove to... serving board. Lay crepes flat to cool. Continue until all the batter is used. Once cooled, crepes can be stacked and stored in a sealable plastic bag in the refrigerator for several days or in the freezer for up to two months. When using frozen crepes, thaw on a rack before gently peeling apart. Savory Variation: Add ¼ teaspoon salt and ¼ cup chopped fresh herbs, spinach or sun dried tomatoes to the egg mixture. Sweet Variation: Add 2 ½ tablespoons sugar, 1 teaspoon vanilla extract and 2 tablespoons of your favorite liqueur to the egg mixture.

Poached Eggs with Spinach and Gruyere Cheese In a Crepe
Makes 10

Ingredients
10 crepes (See previous recipe)
1 package fresh spinach
1 cup sliced fresh mushrooms
4 ounces Gruyere cheese, grated
½ cup olive oil
4 tablespoons butter, divided

Directions
Melt the butter in a skillet over medium heat and add olive oil. Add mushrooms and cheese then set aside. Spread spinach mixture over crepe. Roll crepe into a rectangle, starting with the long side. Repeat procedure with remaining crepes and spinach mixture. Place on lightly greased baking sheets. Bake for 2 to 3 minutes, or until cheese melts. Poach eggs in salted water or poach pan. Place one egg on each folded crepe. Top with Hollandaise sauce.

Hollandaise Sauce

Ingredients
3 egg yolks
2 sticks unsalted butter
1 tablespoon cold water

1 tablespoon lemon juice
Salt and white pepper - to taste

Directions

In the top of a double boiler, whisk the egg yolks until they become thick and sticky. Whisk in the water and lemon juice.

Place the pan or bowl over a saucepan of simmering, not boiling water. Whisk until mixture is warm, about 2 minutes. The yolk mixture has thickened enough when you see the bottom of the pan between strokes and mixture forms a light cream on the wires of the whip. If mixture appears to become lumpy, dip pan immediately in a bowl of ice water to cool. Whisk until smooth and then continue recipe. While whisking the yolk mixture add the pieces of butter, a tablespoon or so at a time, whisking thoroughly to incorporate before adding more butter. As the mixture begins to thicken and become creamy, the butter can be added more rapidly. Season the sauce with salt, white pepper and lemon juice. To keep the sauce warm, set the pan or bowl in lukewarm water or thermos.

Farmhouse Boiled Eggs

Directions

Always use fresh farm eggs. Remove from refrigerator for 2 hours. Add 1 cup of wine vinegar per quart of water. Bring water temperature to 185 degrees. Put eggs into water for 6 minutes. Remove eggs to a chilled water bath for 10 minutes. Gently tap each egg against hard surface without breaking open. Rinse under COLD water and keep in ice water until you need to use them.

Fresh Heirloom Tomato Quiche
Serves 6

Ingredients

4 heirloom tomatoes
1- 9 inch deep dish pie crust unbaked
¾ cup Parmesan cheese, shredded
¾ cup green onions, chopped
2 tablespoons all-purpose flour
½ cup fresh mushrooms, quartered

2 eggs
Dash of cayenne pepper
½ cup half and half

Directions

Preheat oven to 400 degrees

Sprinkle pie crust with 2 tablespoons of cheese and half the onions. Cut tomatoes in chunks. Roll in flour. Place tomatoes in pie crust. Sprinkle with salt and pepper. Put half the remaining cheese on tomatoes. Add mushrooms, cayenne, and remaining onion. In a bowl, beat eggs and cream. Pour over tomato mixture. Sprinkle with remaining cheese. Bake for 40 minutes.

Harvest Granola
Makes 8 cups

Ingredients

4 cups old fashioned rolled oats
1 cup almonds
¾ cup sunflower seeds
¾ cup green pumpkin seeds
¾ cup unsweetened coconut
3 tablespoons sesame seeds
2 tablespoons wheat germ
½ cup butter
½ cup honey
1 cup mixed dried fruit
¾ cup dried bananas

Directions

Preheat oven to 325 degrees. In a large bowl combine dry ingredients, except for the dried fruit. In small pan melt butter and honey over low heat stirring constantly. Pour butter mixture over oat mixture. Stir until well combined. Spread granola on baking pan coated with non-stick spray. Bake for 15 minutes at 325 degrees. Stir granola half way through baking time. Bake until golden brown. Cool in pan on rack. Stir in dried fruits. Delicious topped with fresh fruit and served with yogurt or milk.

Appetizers

Abby J's Mexican Bean and Jalapeño Salsa Pinwheels
Serves 12

Ingredients
1 package spinach tortillas
1 package cream cheese
¾ cup *Abby J's Blackhawk Bean and Jalapeño Salsa*
½ teaspoon garlic salt
½ teaspoon chili powder
½ cup finely chopped black olives
¼ cup green onions
3 tablespoons chopped cilantro

Directions
Combine cream cheese, salsa, green onions, chili powder, olives and chopped cilantro. If you prefer something with less heat, substitute *Abby J's Bean and Jalapeño Salsa for the Black Bean and Herb Salsa.* Spread a thin layer on tortillas.

Roll up tortillas and wrap each one in plastic wrap. Place in freezer to set. Remove from freezer 30 minutes before serving and cut into half-inch slices.

Spicy Kale Chips
Serves 4

Ingredients
6 cups kale leaves, remove rib
4 tablespoons Oliver Farm Infused herb oil or sesame oil
3 tablespoons sesame seeds
1 tablespoon soy sauce

Directions
Preheat oven to 275 degrees. In a large bowl, tear the kale into chip size pieces by holding onto the leaf and tearing downward. Set aside.

In a separate small bowl, mix all the ingredients except the sesame seeds. Pour the marinade over the kale, using your hands work it into the kale.

Sprinkle kale with sesame seeds and lightly toss to coat the leaves.

Lay parchment paper on a cookie sheet. Spread kale out on pan. Making sure the kale is not overlapping, so that it bakes evenly. Bake for 10 minutes. Turn the cookie sheet and bake for another 12-15 minutes. Let chips cool for 3 minutes. The kale will continue to cook after it cools.

Abby J's Mexican Bean and Jalapeño Salsa Pinwheels

Photo > Wade Collins

Abby J's Nachos
Serves 8

Ingredients
11 cups tortilla chips
1 15 ½-ounce can refried, black or pinto beans
1 10-ounce bag frozen corn, thawed
1 pint cherry tomatoes
1 ½ cups sharp cheddar cheese
1 ½ cups Monterey Jack cheese
1 ripe avocado, peeled and chopped
½ cup red onion
½ cup chopped cilantro
3 tablespoons fresh lime juice
2 tablespoons Oliver Farm Infused Sunflower Oil
½ teaspoon ground cumin
½ teaspoon finely grated lime zest
Pickled jalapeño slices
Kosher salt and pepper (to taste)
Abby J's Blackhawk Smokin' Hot Gourmet Sauce

Directions
Preheat oven to 375 degrees. On a rimmed baking sheet, toss the corn with 1 tablespoon of the sunflower oil and season with salt and pepper. Spread the corn into a single layer and roast for 15 minutes, tossing halfway through, until it begins to caramelize. Transfer the roasted corn to a bowl.

Combine the refried beans with the cumin and lime zest. In a medium bowl, combine the tomatoes with the onion, cilantro, 2 tablespoons of the lime juice and the remaining 1 tablespoon of oil. Season the salsa with salt and pepper.

Lightly grease a large rimmed baking sheet and arrange the tortilla chips into a single layer. Top with the refried beans and cheese and bake for 10 minutes or until the cheese is melted and begins to turn brown. In a small bowl, mash the avocado with the remaining 1 tablespoon of lime juice. Season with salt and pepper. Top the chips with the roasted corn, salsa, guacamole and jalapeño slices. Serve with Abby J's hot sauce on the side.

Deviled Eggs
Serves 6

Ingredients
12 hard boiled eggs, peeled, cooled and halved
½ cup Duke's Mayonnaise
1 tablespoon finely chopped watermelon rind pickle
1 ½ teaspoons yellow mustard
¼ teaspoon dill weed
Salt and pepper (to taste)

Directions
Mash yolks with fork. Mix in all other ingredients—get to the texture of hummus. Add more or less mayonnaise to correct the texture. Fill each egg white half with yolk mixture. Top with a sprinkle of dill weed and paprika.

Abby J's Horseradish Deviled Eggs
Serves 6

Ingredients
12 large eggs
½ cup Duke's Mayonnaise
1 tablespoon minced shallot
1 teaspoon horseradish
1 teaspoon Dijon mustard
1 teaspoon dill
1 teaspoon *Abby J's Blackhawk Smokin Hot Sauce*
1 teaspoon salt
Dash of paprika

Directions
Prepare eggs according to the "Perfect, Soft Farmhouse Boiled Eggs" recipe. Remove eggs from pot, and put them in cold water to cool— they will be easier to peel! Peel the eggs, cut in half and remove the yolks. Combine the yolks with the ingredients and fill the eggs. Put a dash of paprika on the filled eggs for garnishing.

Photo > Wade Collins

Abby J's Deviled Eggs

Abby J's Jalapeño Pimento Cheese
Serves 6

Ingredients
16 ounces sharp cheddar cheese
7 ounces diced pimentos
½ cup diced Vidalia onion
3 tablespoons Duke's Mayonnaise
4 tablespoons diced jalapeños
1 teaspoon garlic powder
1 teaspoon salt

Directions
Shred cheese in food processor or by hand. Add pimento, mayo, jalapeños, onions, salt and garlic. Blend only enough to thoroughly combine ingredients. Will keep in refrigerator for up to two weeks.

Pimento Cheese
Serves 6

Ingredients
1 ½ cups Duke's Mayonnaise
8 ounces extra sharp cheddar cheese
8 ounces sharp cheddar cheese
1 cup chopped pecans
1 4-ounce jar diced drained pimentos
½ cup finely grated onion
1 teaspoon Worcestershire sauce
¼ teaspoon cayenne pepper

Directions
Preheat oven to 350 degrees. In a shallow pan, bake pecans in a single layer for 8 to 10 minutes or until toasted and fragrant, stirring halfway through.

In a large bowl, stir together mayo, pimentos, Worcestershire sauce, onion and cayenne pepper until blended.

Finely shred 8 ounces of the cheese, and coarsely shred the other 8 ounces. Add cheese and pecans to mayo mixture.

Mushroom Pesto Crostini
Serves 12

Ingredients
36 slices (½ inch-thick) baguette bread
1 ½ cups fresh Italian parsley
8 ounces white button mushrooms, quartered
¾ cup olive oil
½ cup toasted walnuts
½ cup freshly grated Parmesan
2 garlic cloves
Salt and freshly ground black pepper to taste

Directions
Combine the mushrooms, walnuts, garlic and parsley in a food processor and pulse until coarsely chopped. While you're processing, gradually add ½ cup of the oil, blending until the mushrooms are finely chopped. Transfer the mushroom mixture to a medium bowl and stir in the Parmesan. Season the pesto with salt and pepper. If not using mushroom pesto right away, cover tightly with plastic wrap to prevent possible discoloration of mushrooms.

Preheat grill pan to medium-high heat. Arrange the bread slices on pan, cut-side down. Brush the remaining ¼ cup of oil over the bread slices. Cook until pale golden and crisp, about 5 minutes. Spread the mushroom pesto over the crostini. Arrange the crostini on a platter and serve.

Marinated Bell Peppers
Serves 8

Ingredients
French bread, thinly sliced
6 medium red bell peppers
½ cup sherry vinegar
4 garlic cloves, sliced
2 sprigs of thyme
6 tablespoons olive oil
2 tablespoons salted capers, rinsed and drained
2 tablespoons of freshly chopped flat-leaf parsley
1 teaspoon cayenne pepper
Sea salt and freshly ground pepper (to taste)

Directions

Broil the peppers slowly until the skins are blistered and black. Transfer to a plastic bag, and let steam. When cool, pull off the skins and membranes. Put the peppers in a strainer set over a bowl to catch the juices, and then cut them in ½ inch strips.

Heat a heavy-based skillet, then add the olive oil, vinegar, thyme, rosemary, garlic, cayenne and pepper juices. Cook over low heat for 2 minutes. Add the peppers, capers, parsley, salt and pepper. Cook for one minute while stirring. Remove from the heat and let cool. Cover and chill overnight.

To serve, return to room temperature and serve peppers on thinly sliced French bread. This dish can be kept in the refrigerator for up to one week.

Italian Stuffed Jalapeños
Serves 6

Ingredients

18 to 25 large jalapeños, halved, seeded and deveined
2 pounds hot, spicy sausage, castings removed
2 cups cream cheese
½ cup minced Vidalia onion
½ cup minced bell pepper
½ cup shredded mozzarella or Italian cheese blend
½ cup Parmesan cheese
3 tablespoons minced garlic
1 tablespoon cooking oil
Salt and pepper (to taste)

Directions

Preheat oven to 350 degrees. Place jalapeños on a sheet tray and roast for 10 minutes. Remove from oven and let cool. Heat the oil in a medium sauté pan. Add the sausage and cook for 7 minutes. Add the onions, garlic and pepper, and cook to soften for about 5 more minutes. Remove sausage mix and place into large bowl. Cool to room temperature, and then add cream cheese and Parmesan. Mix ingredients and season with salt and pepper. Place 1 tablespoon of mixture into each jalapeño half, and top with mozzarella cheese. Place in oven and broil until cheese turns brown.

Abby J's Smokin Hot Stuffed Jalapeños
Serves 6

Ingredients

18 to 25 large jalapeños
1 package cream cheese
1 cup Mexican cheese
1 cup *Abby J's Blackhawk Bean and Jalapeño Salsa*
1 cup chopped fresh basil
½ cup minced onion
2 cloves minced garlic

Directions

Preheat the grill. Mix the cream cheese, Mexican cheese, salsa, basil, onion and garlic together until mixture is soft.

Slice the stem off each jalapeño and core out the seeds. Keep the stem, so you can add it back in after filling each jalapeño. Using pastry bag or your choice of tools, fill each jalapeño until it is full. Be careful not to overfill as the filling may spew out during cooking. After you fill the pepper, put the stem back on.

Place each pepper inside a jalapeño steel tray and place on the grill. Grill until peppers are lightly roasted, about 15 minutes on medium heat.

Abby J's Italian Sausage Starters
Serves 4

Ingredients

1 package Italian sausage stuffed with Fontina cheese—you can find all flavors of Italian sausage at your local grocery store!
1 jar *Abby J's Blackhawk Chipotle Peach Salsa*

Directions

Grill sausage on the Big Green Egg. Slice cooked sausage into pieces. Serve with *Abby J's Chipotle Peach Salsa*.

Blackhawk Chili Cheese Puffs

Serves 6

Ingredients:

6 eggs
¼ cup all purpose flour
½ teaspoon baking powder
¾ cup small curd cottage cheese
1 ½ cups Mexican cheese, shredded
1 jar - 2 ounce pimentos, diced
1 can 4 ounces chillies, diced
2 Tablespoons *Abby J's Smokin Hot Sauce*
Salt and Pepper to taste

Directions:

Preheat oven to 350 degrees. In mixing bowl combine all ingredients. Mix well. Pour into 9 inch pie dish. Cover and refrigerate over night. Take out next morning and bake for 60 minutes at 350 degrees. Remove from oven and let cool on rack for 10 minutes before serving. You can top off with *Abby J's Blackhawk Bean & Jalapeño Salsa* for a richer flavor.

Abby J's Olive and Roasted Cherry Tomato Tapenade

Makes 2 ½ Cups

Ingredients

1 cup of fresh cherry tomatoes, quartered
2 teaspoons of minced garlic
2 teaspoons chopped fresh rosemary
1 tablespoon extra-virgin olive oil
Salt and freshly ground pepper, to taste
2 teaspoons chopped fresh basil
2 teaspoons chopped fresh flat-leaf parsley
2 cups Kalamata olives, pitted
1 anchovy, drained and rinse if packed in salt
1 tablespoon freshly squeezed lemon juice
¼ cup extra-virgin olive oil
¼ teaspoon freshly ground pepper

Directions:

Preheat oven to 400 degrees.
In a small baking dish, combine the tomatoes with the garlic, rosemary and olive oil; toss to combine and season with salt & pepper. Evenly spread the tomatoes in a single laker in the dish. Place in the oven and roast for 20 minutes or until tender.

Combine the olives, anchovy, basil and parsley in the bowl of a food processor; pulse until coarsely chopped and well blended. Add the lemon juice, olive oil and pepper, and pulse to incorporate. Transfer to a medium mixing bowl, and add the roasted tomatoes; toss gently to combine. Place the tapenade in a small serving bowl. Store, tightly covered, in the refrigerator. This fresh good-for-you mixture can be used as a garnish or condiment for fish or grilled meats. This also makes a delightful canape served on toasted French bread. Will keep up to a week in the refrigerator.

Springer Mountain Chicken Smokin' Hot Wings

Serves 6

Ingredients

2 dozen Springer Mountain Wings
1 tablespoons garlic
¾ cup *Abby J's Smoking Hot Sauce*
Dash of salt and pepper

Directions

Marinate wings with garlic, sauce, salt and pepper. Refrigerate overnight. Set the Big Green Egg with indirect heat at 325 degrees and make sure you oil your cooking surface. Take chicken out of the refrigerator and place on the grate. Grill on one side for 25 minutes and turn and grill on other side. Bast with hot sauce again the last 5 minutes of cook time, Take off and let cool for 10 minutes and serve with *Abby J's Smokin Hot Sauce* or your favorite dip.

Springer Mountain Chicken ~ Smokin' Hot Wings

My family has been in the poultry business for years. I can remember my grandmother having one of the first chicken houses in Habersham County. Broilers are Georgia's largest agricultural commodity. I truly appreciate all of the local chicken farmers have provided so much for our community.

Springer Mountain Farms chicken is the only chicken I cook. It is truly the best chicken on the market. Their chickens are all natural and are fed a vegetarian diet with vitamins, minerals and fresh mountain water. They contain no antibiotics or growth stimulants.

Photo used with permission from Big Green Egg. Photo > Nancy Suttles

Salads

Farmhouse Pear and Radish Salad

Serves 8

White Balsamic Vinaigrette Ingredients

2 tablespoons shallots, minced
1 cup extra virgin olive oil
½ cup balsamic vinegar
Kosher salt and freshly ground pepper (To taste)

Salad Ingredients

20 radishes, quartered
8 radishes, shaved and placed in ice water to crisp
8 pears, quartered
6 ounces arugula salad mix
½ pound green grapes, quartered
½ pound of Gorgonzola cheese

Directions

Prepare vinaigrette by marinating shallots in vinegar for 20 minutes. Then slowly whisk in olive oil and season to taste.

Mix all salad ingredients and season and toss with the White Balsamic Vinaigrette. Top with Gorgonzola

Spinach Salad

Serves 4

Ingredients

8 hard-boiled eggs, sliced
8 cups spinach
2 cucumbers, cut lengthwise into eights
4 cups chopped tomatoes
3 cups shredded carrots
2 cups Parmesan cheese
1 cup candied walnuts
1 cup almonds

Directions

Divide the spinach between four large salad bowls.

Divide the tomatoes up on one side of each bowl, and do the same with the carrots but on the opposite side. Between the two vegetables, arrange two of the sliced boiled eggs.

In the center of each salad form a star with the cucumbers, leaving the center open to top with the candied walnuts and almonds.

Sprinkle ½ cup of Parmesan over each salad. Serve with Red Wine Mustard Vinaigrette Dressing.

Grilled Corn and Black Bean Salad

Serves 6

Ingredients

3 ears shucked corn
1 15-ounce can black beans drained
½ cup fresh lime juice
½ cup minced red onion
3 tablespoons white vinegar
2 tablespoons minced fresh cilantro
1 tablespoon *Abby J's Blackhawk Smokin Hot Sauce*
2 teaspoons sugar
2 teaspoons ground cumin
Lime wedges

Directions

Prepare the grill. Place corn on grill rack, and grill until corn is lightly browned, turning every 3 to 4 minutes. Let cool.

Cut kernels from corn and place in a bowl. Add juice and the remaining items except lime wedges, stir and combine. Chill for 1 hour. Garnish with the lime wedges and serve.

This recipe is excellent as a side or served over baked tortilla chips! Can be stored in refrigerator for up to one week.

Photo > Wade Collins

Red Wine Mustard Vinaigrette Dressing

Ingredients
2 cups red wine vinegar
1 ½ cups spicy brown mustard
1 cup olive oil
¾ cup packed brown sugar
1 tablespoon lemon pepper
¼ teaspoon salt

Directions
In a large bowl, combine all the ingredients. Whisk for 2 minutes and serve over salad. Can be stored in refrigerated for up to 2 weeks.

The Blackhawk "Iceburg Wedge" with Blue Cheese Dressing
Serves 8

Salad Ingredients
2 heads fresh iceberg lettuce, quartered
1 4-ounce container crumbled blue cheese
6 slices bacon, cooked until crisp and chopped coarsely
1 medium tomato, chopped
1 medium red onion, diced

Chunky Blue Cheese Dressing Ingredients
1 4-ounce container crumbled blue cheese
½ cup Duke's mayonnaise
½ cup sour cream
¼ cup milk
2 teaspoon lemon juice
½ teaspoon salt

Directions
Put dressing ingredients in a blender and process until smooth. Place wedge on plate and drizzle blue cheese dressing on each wedge. Sprinkle with onions, cheese, tomato and bacon.

Marinated Pepper Salad
Serves 4

Ingredients
2 red bell peppers, quartered
2 yellow bell peppers, quartered
8 tablespoons olive oil
2 tablespoons balsamic vinegar
2 tablespoons water
2 garlic cloves, thinly sliced
4 sprigs thyme
4 tablespoons of parsley, leaves picked
1 cup basil leaves
2 cups watercress
4 ounces Pecorino, shaved
2 tablespoons drained capers
salt and pepper to taste

Directions:
Preheat the oven to 375 degrees. Toss the peppers with 1 tablespoon of the oil and a dash of salt. Roast in a roasting pan for 35 to 40 minutes or until they soften. Remove to a bowl and cover with plastic wrap. Once cooled to room temperature, peel the peppers and cut into thick strips. Whisk together 2 tablespoons of the oil, balsamic vinegar, water, thyme, garlic and a dash of salt and pepper. Pour this over the peppers and put into refrigerator for at least an hour. To assemble the salad, toss together the herbs watercress, drained pepper strips, Pecorino and capers. Add the remaining 1 tablespoon of olive oil and add more if desired.

Spicy Caprese Rice Salad
Serves 4

Ingredients
3 tablespoons olive oil
1 tablespoons balsamic vinegar
½ cup fresh basil chopped
1 medium Vidalia onion diced
6 ounces mozzarella cheese fresh cut into chunks

1 cup fresh vine ripe cherry tomatoes
1 teaspoons salt
1 teaspoon ground fresh pepper
½ cup diced jalapeños
1 cup basmati rice

Directions
In a large bowl combine 2 tablespoons herb oil, vinegar, basil, tomatoes, mozzarella, salt, and pepper. Set aside to marinate and cook the rice. Heat the herb oil in a medium saucepan and add onion and jalapeños. Cook until softened, about 3 to 5 minutes. Add rice and 1 ¾ cups water and bring to a boil, cover and simmer until water is absorbed, about 20 minutes. Toss rice mixture with tomato mixture, serve warm. Great side dish for pork!

Abby J's Special Dressing

Ingredients
2 oz. can anchovies
½ medium Vidalia onion
1 rib of celery
1 teaspoon black pepper
1 heaping teaspoon accent
½ teaspoon sugar
¼ cup mustard
1 teaspoon lemon juice
1 clove garlic
3 eggs
2 cups safflower oil

Mix all but last two ingredients in blender. Add eggs then oil ¼ cup at a time. Chill and serve with green salads. This is especially nice with Caesar salad.

Jalapeño Cilantro Vinaigrette

Ingredients
2 Jalapeños
2 cups cilantro
1 cup extra virgin olive oil
½ cup white wine vinegar
1 teaspoon Dijon mustard
2 tablespoons fresh lime juice
1 tablespoon fresh lemon juice
2 cloves garlic
½ teaspoon sea salt

Remove the stem and seeds from the jalapeño and mince in a food processor or blender then add the garlic and mince. Scrape the sees at least once with a spatula. Measure then add all other ingredients and blend together well. I love using cilantro because it is an extreme antioxidant booster that helps detoxify the body. It also helps to promote a healthy liver and lowers blood sugar.

Mains

Chipotle Peach Grilled Chicken Breasts
Serves 8

Ingredients:
8 Springer Mountain bone-in Chicken Breast Halves

Marinade Ingredients
½ cup olive oil
½ cup *Abby J's Chipotle Peach Salsa*
1 onion, chopped onion
1 teaspoon salt
1 teaspoon black pepper
2 garlic cloves
2 teaspoons paprika
1 teaspoon cumin
Juice of 2 limes

Directions
Put ingredients in food processor and liquify.
Put marinade in a gallon-size bag and add chicken breast halves.
Refrigerate for at least 5 hours. Remove chicken from marinade and place on grill. Grill, turning occasionally, until chicken is throughly cooked. This normally takes 20 to 25 minutes on medium heat.

Fresh Egg Salad Sandwich
Makes 4

Ingredients:
8 hard-cooked eggs, peeled
3 tablespoons of Duke's Mayonnaise
1 tablespoon of minced jalapeños
½ teaspoon honey mustard
½ teaspoon black pepper
½ teaspoon garlic powder
1 pinch salt
8 slices of Italian bread
24 leaves baby spinach
8 slices heirloom tomatoes

Directions
In a medium bowl, mash the hard-cooked eggs with a fork. Mix in the mayonnaise, honey mustard and jalapeño. Season with black pepper, garlic powder, and salt.

Spread onto bread and add spinach and tomatoes and top with remaining bread.

Photo > Wade Collins

Lodge Cast Iron
Smokin' Hot Pork Chops with
Grilled Pineapple

Serves 5

Ingredients:
5 pork chops ½ inch to 1 inch thick
2 tablespoons Oliver Farm infused herb
sunflower oil
2 tablespoons *Abby J's Smokin Hot Sauce*
1 teaspoon salt
1 teaspoon pepper
2 tablespoons cooking oil
1 pineapple sliced ½ inch thick

Directions:
Marinate pork chops in sunflower oil, hot
sauce salt and pepper for 30 minutes.
Heat cast iron skillet to 375 degrees with
the cooking oil and cook 5 to 7 minutes on
each side until seared.

Grill the sliced pineapples and add them on
top of the pork chops. Serve hot and enjoy.

Abby J's Black Bean & Herb Stuffed Peppers
Serves 8

Ingredients:
½ pound lean ground beef
½ pound hot sausage
¾ cup Vidalia onions, chopped
1 cup *Abby J's Black Bean & Herb Salsa*
1 cup cooked rice
1 cup refried beans
1 cup corn
1 jalapeño, chopped
2 tablespoons chopped fresh parsley
3 garlic cloves, chopped
½ cup chopped basil
1 teaspoon cumin
1 cup Mexican cheese

Directions:
Cut bell pepper in half lengthwise from top of stem to bottom; remove and discard seeds and membranes. Place in pot of boiling water for 3 minutes. Remove and drain on paper towel.
In medium skillet cook meats and onion. Add all ingredients and simmer for 10 minutes. Place peppers in 13 x 9 x 2-inch baking dish; stuff peppers with meat and refried bean mixture. Cover dish with foil and bake at 350 degrees for 40 minutes. Uncover and top each pepper with shredded cheese. Continue until cheese is lightly brown.

Rib Eye Steak with Chanterelle Mushrooms & Bordelaise Sauce
Ingredients:
2 to 2 ½ pounds of rib-eye steak
kosher Salt and freshly ground pepper
cooking oil
4 Tablespoons of unsalted Butter

Bordelaise Sauce
1 cup red wine

¼ cup shallots
½ cup carrots
¼ cup mushrooms
10 sprigs Italian Parsley
2 sprigs Thyme
2 bay leaves
10 peppercorns
2 tablespoons sliced garlic
1 cup chicken stock

Chanterelle Mushrooms
2 tablespoon unsalted butter
1 tablespoon of garlic
2 cups chanterelle mushrooms cleaned and cut into pieces
Kosher salt and freshly ground pepper

Sprinkle the steak with salt and pepper and allow to stay in refrigerator overnight. Before cooking remove the meat from refrigerator and allow to be brought to room temperature.

Bordelaise Sauce
In a medium saucepan, bring the wine, parsley, thyme, bay leaf and garlic to a simmer. Simmer until all liquid is evaporated. Add the peppercorns and chicken stock. Simmer for 10 to 15 minutes or until the stock is reduced to a sauce consistency (about ½ cup). Strain sauce through a mesh strainer and refrigerate for 2 to 3 days. For the chanterelle mushrooms: Heat the butter and garlic over medium heat. Add the mushrooms, season with salt and pepper and cook for about 5 minutes. Grill the steaks on the Big Green Egg to medium rare and remove. Heat sauce and pour over the mushrooms and steak.

Smokin' Hot Garlic Shrimp
Serves 4

Ingredients
48 medium uncooked shrimp, deveined, with tail on
6 tablespoons extra-virgin olive oil
10 garlic cloves, bruised
4 tablespoons *Abby J's Smokin' Hot Sauce*

8 small fresh bay leaves
Juice of one lemon
sea salt

Directions

To prepare the shrimp, put them on a plate and sprinkle lightly with salt. Heat the olive oil and add the garlic in a skillet and fry until brown. Add the bay leaves, *Abby J's Smokin' Hot Sauce*, and shrimp all at once and fry without turning until the shrimp are crusted and curl on one side, then turn them over and crust the other side, about 3 to 4 minutes in total. Serve immediately while *"Smokin Hot"!*

Collard & Mustard Greens with Ham Hocks

Serves 8

Ingredients

3 bunches -3 lbs. mixed collard greens, and Mustard Greens, rinsed and chopped
2 tablespoons of vegetable oil
2 ham hocks 1 ½ lbs.
1 Vidalia onion, chopped
2 gloves garlic, minced
1 jalapeño diced
1 bay leaf
½ teaspoon dried thyme
½ teaspoon cayenne pepper
2 teaspoon salt
¼ cup cider vinegar
3 cans (14 ½ ounces each) chicken broth

Directions:

In a large stockpot heat oil over medium heat. Add ham hocks, onion, and jalapeño; cook until onion has softened, about 10 minutes. Add greens; cook stirring frequently, until wilted, about 8 minutes. Add broth, 6 cups of water, garlic, bay leaf, and thyme; season with salt and cayenne pepper. Bring to a boil; reduce to a simmer and cook for 2 ½ hours or until ham hocks are tender and the greens are very tender. Remove ham hocks from pot; shred meat, discarding skin and bones. Remove bay leaf and season with salt.

Abby J's Chile Relleno Strata

Serves 8

Ingredients

12 eggs beaten
1 -12 ounce can whole green chilies
2 cups monterey jack cheese, grated
½ cup milk
½ cup half & half cream
1 teaspoon salt
2 tablespoons *Abby J's Smokin' Hot Sauce*

Directions

Preheat oven to 350 degrees. In a well-greased quiche pan layer half the chilies on the bottom so the ends point to the center of the pan. Cover with cheese and remaining chilies. Mix eggs, cream, milk, and hot sauce together. Pour over chilies. Bake for 60 minutes or until strata is set.

Spicy Chicken Quesadillas

Serves 6

Ingredients

2 cups chopped Springer Mountain Chicken
1 cup of chopped Roma tomatoes
1 ½ cup pepper jack cheese
3 green onions finely chopped
1 jalapeño diced
1 teaspoon cumin
1 teaspoon garlic salt
2 teaspoons chili powder
8 flour tortillas (8-inch)
Oliver Farm infused herb oil

Directions

Preheat oven to 350 degrees. Mix chicken, cheese, tomato, green onions, jalapeño, chili powder, cumin, and garlic salt. Place 4 tortillas on ungreased baking sheet. Spread ¼ of the chicken mixture evenly on each tortilla. Top with remaining tortillas. Lightly brush with Oliver Farm infused herb oil. Bake 5 to 10 minutes or just until cheese is melted. Cut into 3-inch wedges. Serve hot.

Photo > Wade Collins

Bow Tie Lasagna

Serves 12

Ingredients

1 box bow tie pasta 12 oz.
1 lb. sweet Italian sausage
1 lb. lean ground beef
1 24 ounce of Italian Tomato Sauce
1 14. 5 ounces diced tomatoes
1 6 o tomato paste
½ cup water
1 Vidalia onion diced
3 garlic cloves minced
2 teaspoons of dried basil
1 teaspoon of fennel seeds
1 teaspoon dried rosemary
½ teaspoon salt
4 tablespoons of fresh chopped parsley
8 ounces ricotta cheese
8 ounces cottage cheese
1 egg
2 cups mozzarella cheese
¾ cup grated Parmesan cheese

Directions

Preheat oven to 375 degrees. In a Lodge cast iron skillet, cook sausage, ground beef, onion, and garlic over medium heat until well browned. Stir in diced tomatoes, tomato paste, tomato sauce and water. Season with salt, basil, fennel seeds, Italian seasoning, pepper, 2 tablespoons parsley and rosemary. Simmer, covered, for about 1 hour, stirring occasionally.

Bring a large pot of lightly salted water to a boil. Cook pasta 12- 14 minutes. Drain pasta, and rinse with cold water. In a mixing bowl, combine ricotta cheese, cottage cheese with egg, remaining parsley. To assemble, spread 1 ½ cups of meat sauce in the bottom of a 9 x 13 inch baking dish. Spread layer of bow tie pasta to cover. Spread with one half of the cheese mixture. Top with a third of mozzarella cheese, and sprinkle with ¼ cup Parmesan cheese. Repeat layers, and top with remaining mozzarella, and Parmesan cheese. Cover with foil: to prevent from sticking spray foil with cooking spray , or make sure foil does not touch cheese. Bake in preheated oven for 25 minutes. Remove foil, and bake for additional 25 minutes. Cool at least 15 minutes before serving.

Lodge Cast Iron

My kitchen is simply not complete without Lodge Cast Iron skillets. I can remember many good times frying chicken in cast iron skillets on the banks of the Soque River. The taste of the chicken and the crispness is something you never will forget ... a true Southern delicacy.

I use my Lodge Cast Iron skillets on a regular basis, and it still satisfies me to know that it cooks evenly—I always get that even crisp and crunch no matter what I am cooking.

I have a growing inventory of Lodge Cast Iron cookware and I have inherited some which I still use. If you maintain and season your cast iron, they will last a lifetime and become a family heirloom.

~ Photo courtesy of Lodge Cast Iron ~

Fresh Summertime Lasagna
Serves 6

Ingredients
1 tablespoon Oliver Farm Infused Herb Oil
¾ cup sliced mushrooms
¾ cup chopped zucchini
½ cup sliced carrots
½ cup sliced red onion
¾ cup chopped red bell pepper
26 ounces of tomato basil sauce
1 tablespoon minced garlic
2 tablespoons pesto
15 ounce ricotta cheese
1 cup mozzarella cheese
14 cup Parmesan cheese
6 ounces cooked lasagna noodles
Fresh basil leaves

Directions
Preheat oven to 375 degrees. Heat oil in a saucepan over medium heat. Add mushrooms and the next four ingredients; cook for 5 minutes stirring frequently. Add pasta sauce and bring to a boil. Reduce heat; simmer 10 minutes. Combine pesto, minced garlic and ricotta in a small bowl. Spread ½ cup tomato mixture in the bottom of a 8-inch square baking dish coated with cooking spray. Arrange four noodle halves over the tomato mixture. Top noodles with half of the ricotta mixture; and 1 cup of tomato mixture sprinkle with mozzarella cheese. Repeat layers, ending with noodles. Add remaining mozzarella with the Parmesan, and spread over the noodles. Cover and bake for 30 minutes. Uncover and bake for additional 20 minutes. Let stand for 20 minutes. Garnish with fresh basil leaves and cherry tomatoes.

Springer Mountain Farms Southern Fried Chicken

Serves 4

Ingredients

1 whole bird, cut into 8 pieces
1 cup milk
1 tablespoon garlic powder
2 large eggs
½ cup milk
1 cup all-purpose flour
1 tablespoon salt
1 tablespoon of seasoned pepper
24 ounces Crisco

Directions

Let chicken stay overnight and marinate in 1 cup of milk and 1 tablespoon of garlic overnight. Remove the chicken and whisk the eggs with the ½ cup milk. In another bowl, whisk the flour with the salt and pepper. Dredge the chicken in the seasoned flour. You can add hot spices in the flour for more flavor. Allow the chicken to dry for about 30 minutes.

In a cast iron skillet, heat the oil to 365 degrees. Add the chicken and fry over moderate heat turning occasionally until the chicken is deeply golden brown and an instant thermometer reads 170 degrees. This takes about 20 to 24 minutes. Drain the chicken on paper towels and serve immediately.

Summer Squash Casserole

Serves 6

Ingredients:

1 ½ pounds of yellow Squash (2 pints)
1 small jar of pimento
1 cup sour cream
1 teaspoon oregano
4 small grated carrots
1 package herb bread stuffing

1 can chicken soup
1 large Vidalia onion chopped fine
1 stick of butter

Directions:

Preheat oven to 350 degrees. Cook squash in salt water until tender. Drain excess water and mash. Add all ingredients and reserve ½ of stuffing mix. Mix well. Line shallow casserole dish with remainder of stuffing that has been mixed with melted butter. Reserve a small amount for topping. Pour squash mixture into dish and sprinkle on topping and bake 30 to 35 minutes.

Herb Roasted Pork Loin

Serves 4

Ingredients

1 ½ lbs. pork loin roast
4 tablespoon cooking oil
1 tsp. ground cinnamon
2 teaspoons ground cumin
1 tsp. cayenne

For the Crust

1 vidalia onion. chopped
3 cloves garlic, smashed
2 tablespoons freshly grated ginger
1 cup fresh cilantro leaves
1 lime zested
2 tablespoons olive oil
¼ cup plain bread crumbs
kosher salt
2 tablespoons Dijon mustard

Directions

Preheat oven to 375 degrees.
In a small bowl, mix together the cinnamon, cumin, cayenne, and salt. Rub the mixture over the outside of the loin to marinate. In a large sauté pan, heat the oil over medium heat and brown the pork

Herb Roasted Pork Loin continued . . .

roast on all sides, just until golden brown. Remove the pork to a sheet tray, fat side up. Make the herb crust: In a food processor, combine the onions, garlic, ginger, cilantro, and lime zest. In the same sauté pan in which the pork was browned, add the olive oil and the onion mixture and cook until softened. Stir in the bread crumbs and cook another 2 minutes. Season with salt to taste. Spread the mustard on top of the fatty layer and then press the herb crust into it and bake until the internal temperature reaches 160 °F, about 30 minutes. Remove to a cutting board and allow to rest 15 minutes

Abby J's Spicy Enchiladas
Serves 8

Sauce Ingredients
1 tablespoon cooking oil
1 tablespoon all-purpose flour
1 28 ounce can enchilada sauce
2 cups chicken broth
½ teaspoon salt
1 teaspoon black pepper
2 tablespoons chopped fresh cilantro

Directions
Combine oil, and flour over medium heat to create a paste and let it turn brown. Add the enchilada sauce, chicken broth, and salt. Bring to a boil, then reduce the heat to low and simmer for about 30-45 minutes. Add in the cilantro.

Meat Ingredients
1 pound lean ground beef
½ pound hot sausage
1 4 ounce can diced chillies
1 large jalapeño diced
½ teaspoon salt
1 teaspoon chili powder
1 teaspoon cumin
1 teaspoon red pepper flakes
!0 flour tortillas

2 cups Mexican cheese
1 cup sharp cheddar cheese
5 green onions chopped
½ cup cilantro chopped

Directions
While the sauce is simmering, brown the pork and beef along with the onions. When cooked through, drain fat. Stir in the chillies, jalapeños, chili powder, ground cumin and red pepper flakes. Preheat the oven to 350 degrees. Pour about ¾ cup of the sauce on the bottom of a 9 x 13 inch casserole dish. Add the meat, cheese and onions. Roll up the tortilla tight in the bottom of the pan. Continue until you have no more tortillas and filling left. Pour remaining sauce over the enchiladas and top with remaining cheddar. Bake for 20 minutes. Garnish with cilantro and fresh green onions.

Vine Ripe Tomato Pie
Serves 6

Ingredients
1 deep pie crust
4 - 5 vine ripe tomatoes
1 large Vidalia onion
1 cup sharp cheddar cheese, grated
1 cup pepper jack cheese, grated
1 cup Duke's mayonnaise
1 habanero diced (optional)
2 cayenne peppers diced (optional)
15 to 20 leaves cinnamon basil
salt, pepper, and garlic powder to taste

Directions
Preheat oven to 325 degrees and bake pie shell covering outer edges with foil for 10 minutes. Mix mayonnaise and sharp cheddar cheese. Season with salt, pepper, and garlic. Thickly slice unpeeled tomatoes and add diced onions and peppers. Layer into pie shell and add basil. Sprinkle each layer with cheese and repeat. Spread mayo and cheese on top and then top with remaining cheese. Bake at 350 degrees for 30 minutes.

Vine Ripe Tomato Pie

North Georgia Gold

Chanterelle mushrooms grow wild on our farm. We start harvesting in July. I love to sauté them in garlic and butter ... they just melt in your mouth!

Abby J's Tuscan Meatloaf

Serves 6

For the decoration inside:
1 boiled carrot sliced length ways in 4 pieces
1 lightly boiled zucchini, slice length ways in 4 pieces
2 hard-boiled eggs

For the meatloaf
1 cup of Italian breadcrumbs to coat
1 lb ground beef
½ lb. Italian sausage
1 cup chanterelle mushrooms chopped
1 teaspoon nutmeg
1 cup parsley
2 cloves garlic, chopped
¼ lb Parmesan cheese
¼ ricotta cheese
2 boiled mashed medium potatoes
3 tablespoons flour
1 glass of white wine

For the sauce
2 lb ripe tomatoes, skinned and chopped
2 cloves garlic
Bunch of basil - 25 leaves

Directions
Preheat the oven to 375 degrees. Mix the ingredients for the meatloaf very well and roll meat out into a dinner plate sized shape. Place the vegetables on the rolled mixture and cut the eggs in half along side the vegetables. Roll into a log shape then add the breadcrumbs on meatloaf. Cook in the oven for 40 minutes or until well browned. Take out of oven.

Make a tomato sauce by cooking the tomatoes slowly with olive oil and garlic, adding the basil at the end and save some basil for garnish. Cook the meatloaf for additional 10 minutes with the tomato sauce and garnish with the basil leaves.

Abby J's Tuscan Meatloaf

Abby J's Famous Chili

Serves 12

Ingredients
1 lb. ground beef
1 lb. hot pork sausage
1 large Vidalia onion diced
1 medium red bell pepper, chopped
1 medium poblano pepper chopped
4 cloves garlic finely chopped
¼ cup hot chili seasoning mix
1 tablespoon ground cumin
2 teaspoons paprika
1 tablespoon dried oregano
1 quart jar of preserved tomatoes (28 ounces of plum tomatoes)
1 16 ounce diced tomatoes
1 12 ounce bottle of amber beer
1 cup chicken broth
1 cup orange juice
1 15 ounce can Dark Red Kidney Beans
1 15 ounce can Northern Beans
3 tablespoons *Abby J's Smokin Hot Sauce*
Shredded sharp cheddar cheese and sliced scallions for topping

Directions
Cook the beef and sausage in a large sauce pan. Drain and set aside. Add the onion, and peppers to a saucepan and cook until soft, about 5 minutes. Add the garlic and 1 teaspoon salt and cook 2 minutes.

In a large stock pot combine cooked meat and peppers and seasonings. Stir together and add tomatoes, beans, beer, broth, and orange juice. Cook, stirring occasionally, until the chili thickens slightly about 1 hour. Stir the hot sauce into the chili and season with salt. Add some chicken broth or more beer if the chili is too thick. Enjoy with Abby J's jalapeño muffins!

Condiments & Sauces

Herb-Shallot Mayonnaise

Ingredients
1 cup mayonnaise
2 tablespoons finely chopped parsley
2 tablespoon Dijon mustard
1 shallot, minced
Salt and Pepper to taste

Incorporate ingredients and put in a pint jar. Place in refrigerator. This will keep for one week.

Basil Mayonnaise

Ingredients:
1 cup Duke's Mayonnaise
1 cup of basil chopped
1 teaspoon kosher salt
¼ teaspoon Black pepper
1 teaspoon lemon juice, freshly squeezed 1 tablespoon olive oil 1 teaspoon garlic, minced

Whisk all these together in a food processor for 20 seconds and then put in pint jar. This will keep up to a week.

Spicy Pesto

Ingredients:
3 cups packed fresh basil leaves
½ cup diced jalapeños
4 cloves garlic
¾ grated Parmesan Cheese
½ cup olive oil
¼ pine nuts

Combine basil garlic, jalapeños, nuts and cheese in a food processor and add the oil as you blend this into a smooth paste. Put this in a pint jar and place in the freezer. You may add more Parmesan cheese to this when you take it out of the freezer as it thaws.

Shallots differ from onions as they are smaller, and grow in clusters of bulbs from each plant-root system. The bulbs are characteristically less pungent than that of onions and garlic, which makes them one of the my favorite ingredients

Pizza

Farm Fresh Roma Tomato Pizza Sauce
Makes 1 Cup

Ingredients
6 medium Roma tomatoes
4 garlic cloves left whole
1 small Vidalia onion
¼ cup extra-virgin olive oil
2 teaspoons of dried basil
1 teaspoon oregano
½ teaspoon crushed red pepper flakes
Salt and freshly ground black pepper, to taste
1 teaspoon sugar
12 teaspoon balsamic vinegar
1 teaspoon chopped fresh basil
1 teaspoon chopped flat-leaf parsley

Directions
Preheat oven to 300 degrees. Place rack in the lower third of oven. Core the tomatoes and slice them lengthwise into quarters. Squeeze each wedge removing the seeds. Cut the onion into 1-inch chunks. Combine the tomatoes, onions, garlic, ¼ of the olive oil, oregano, basil and crushed red pepper in a medium mixing bowl. Season with salt and pepper. Mix all the ingredients well and spread them evenly on baking sheet.

Bake until the onions and garlic have caramelized and the tomatoes have released their juices, about 1 to 1 ½ hours. Remove from oven and let cool for 10 to 15 minutes. Transfer tomato mixture into food processor. Add sugar and balsamic vinegar to the tomato mixture.

Process until it is completely pureed. If sauce is to thick simply add more olive oil. Add the fresh herbs and pulse to combine and season with salt and pepper. Cool completely and store tightly in covered container for up to one week in the refrigerator.

Pizza Dough
3 ¼ cups all-purpose
2 tablespoons Olive Oil
2 tablespoons Oliver Farms Infused Sunflower Oil
1 teaspoon salt
1 ½ cups warm water
½ teaspoon brown sugar
2 ¼ active dry yeast

In a large bowl, dissolve the yeast and brown stage in the water, and let sit for 10 minutes. Stir the salt and oil into the yeast solution. Mix in 2 ½ cups of the flour. Turn dough out onto a clean, well floured surface, and knead in more flour until the dough is not sticky. Place the dough into a bowl with the sunflower oil, cover with a cloth.

Let the dough rise until double; this should take about an hour. Punch down the dough, and form a tight ball. Allow the dough to relax for a minute before rolling out.

If you are baking your pizza in a pan, lightly oil the pan with infused oil, let the dough rise for 15 to 20 minutes before topping and baking it.

Photo > Wade Collins

Abby J's Chipotle Peach Pizza

Serves 4

Ingredients:
1 pizza dough
½ cup Oliver Farms Infused Sunflower Oil
¼ cup Parmesan cheese
¾ cup *Abby J's Chipotle Peach Salsa*
½ cup sliced green onions
½ cup slice black olives
½ cup mushrooms sliced
2 tablespoons cilantro (chopped)
3 ounces pepperoni
¾ cup Italian cheese
½ cup of Mexican cheese
¼ cup diced jalapeños (optional)

Directions:
Preheat oven or Green Egg to to 400 degrees. Remove dough from freezer and allow to rise while adding the sunflower oil on dough on the pizza pan. This will take at least 2 hours.

After dough has risen add Parmesan cheese directly on the pan. Start spreading the dough to form crust. Spread *Abby J's Peach Salsa* on crust and add next 7 ingredients then top with cheese and jalapeños if you like spicy. Bake for 18 to 20 minutes.

Smoked Gouda & Vegetable Pizza

Ingredients
Basic pizza dough - see page 60
10 spears asparagus
1 can of small salad cut artichokes
1 red bell pepper, cored and sliced thin
Small bunch of arugula
olive oil
salt and pepper
2 ounces smoked gouda cut into chunks

Directions
Heat grill to high. Toss sliced vegetables, except for leafy greens, in olive oil and season with salt and pepper. Grill vegetables until lightly charred on both sides. Layer all ingredients except for arugula and place on grill. Lower heat to medium. Let the crust brown and the cheese melt. Top with arugula, cut into wedges and serve immediately. Garnish with fresh basil.

Steak, Gorgonzola & Scallion Pizza

Ingredients
¼ cup plus 3 tablespoons olive oil
2 garlic cloves, minced
1 teaspoon freshly ground black pepper
10 ounces grilled beef, thinly sliced
Flour (for dusting)
Basic pizza dough - see page 60
8 medium spring onions
4 leaves of fresh Italian oregano
2 ounces Gorgonzola cheese, cut into thumb-size chunks
½ cup of Fontina cheese
10 fresh basil leaves, chopped

Directions
Grill steak on the Big Green Egg for 12–15 minutes per side for medium-rare to medium. Remove and let rest for 5–10 minutes. Thinly slice the steak across the grain.

In a small bowl, combine ¼ cup olive oil, garlic and pepper. Add meat and turn a few times to coat in marinade. Cover and refrigerate overnight.

Heat oven to 425 degrees. Brush dough with olive oil and place on the preheated baking stone Bake for 5 minutes. Remove dough from stone, and top with other ingredients, leaving a border around edges for crust to brown.

Place the assembled pizza back on the baking stone for 10 -15 minutes, or until the crust is nicely browned on the bottom. Cut into wedges and serve immediately, garnished with additional fresh oregano, if desired.

Steak, Gorgonzola & Scallion Pizza

Photo reprinted with permission from Big Green Egg, Cooking Tips + Techniques, Pizza Basics. Photo by Nancy Suttles
www.biggreenegg.com/publications

Heirloom Tomato Pizza

Serves 6

Ingredients

1 pizza dough - see recipe on page 60
2 tbsp Oliver Farm infused herb oil
½ pound low-fat ricotta
2 tsp lemon zest
½ tsp kosher salt
½ tsp pepper
1 ½ pound heirloom tomatoes, sliced
12 slices of pepperoni
½ cup diced bell peppers
1 tbsp chopped fresh chives
1 tbsp fresh basil, torn
1 tsp fresh rosemary
3 tbsp grated Parmesan

Directions

Heat oven to 425 degrees. Drizzle large pizza pan with 1 tablespoon of the oil. Roll dough in oil and let rise. Stretch over pan and add 1 tablespoon of Parmesan under crust.

Bake until crust is golden, about 8 minutes. Whisk together the ricotta, lemon zest, 1 tablespoon oil, ½ tsp salt, ½ teaspoon of pepper.

Spread over crust and top with heirloom tomatoes.

Bake until cheese begins to brown. Garnish with chives, rosemary, basil and 2 tablespoons of Parmesan.

1/2 heirloom tomato pizza, 1/2 pepperoni

Sides

Simple Roasted Butternut Squash
Serves 4

1 butternut squash- peeled seeded and cut into 1 inch cubes
2 tbsp olive oil
2 cloves garlic, minced
Salt and pepper to taste

Preheat oven to 400 degrees. Toss butternut squash with olive oil and garlic in a large bowl. Season with salt and black pepper. Place squash on a coated baking sheet. Roast in the preheated one until squash is tender and browned, 25 to 30 minutes.

Photo > Wade Collins

Abby J's Pasta Salad
Serves 8

Ingredients
1 16 ounce of angel hair pasta
1 tablespoon Accent
1 tablespoon garlic
2 tablespoons seasoning salt
3 tablespoons lemon juice
4 tablespoons light olive oil
1 cup of duke's mayo
½ cup onion, finely chopped
½ cup green pepper, finely chopped
½ cup green olives
½ cup black olives

Directions
Cook pasta according to directions and drain pasta after it is cooked. Combine all other ingredients and then add pasta and mix well. This side dish is fabulous with pork, beef, and chicken.

Chipotle Peach Baked Vidalia Onions
Serves 4

Ingredients
4 onions/core the middle out
6/8 small squash sliced ½ inch thick
6 tablespoons of *Abby J's Chipotle Peach Salsa*
½ cup Pepper Jack cheese
½ cup Parmesan Cheese
½ cup olive oil

Directions
Put onions and squash in microwave for 5 minutes to reduce baking time. Take out and add salsa to each onion and then top with cheeses. Add squash and olive oil to baking dish and bake for 40 minutes. Fabulous dish and low calorie. A meal in itself.

Herbed Mashed Potatoes
Serves 6

Ingredients
4 lbs. Yukon Potatoes cut into 1 inch cubes
½ cup unsalted butter cut into small pieces
½ cup sour cream
Salt to taste
½ cup fresh herbs, chives, dill & tarragon
1 cup half and half (heated)
freshly ground pepper

Directions
Combine the potatoes, 2 teaspoons salt, and water to cover by 2 inches. Bring to a rapid boil, reduce the heat to medium, and cook, uncovered, until tender about 20 to 25 minutes.
Drain the potatoes and transfer them to a large bowl. Using a potato masher, mash them while they are still hot.
Add the sour cream, butter, and herbs to the potatoes and slowly pour in the hot half and half while stirring with a wooden spoon. Continue to stir until the potatoes are light and creamy. Season to taste with salt and pepper. Serve at once.

Macaroni & Cheese with Spicy Sausage
Serves 4-6

Ingredients
½ lb. elbow macaroni
1 lb. spicy pork sausage
3 cups sharp cheddar cheese
9 tablespoons unsalted butter
3 cups whole milk
1 cup Vidalia onion chopped
½ cup green bell pepper chopped
½ cup flour
1 tablespoon garlic, minced
1 teaspoon anise
¼ cup butter
½ breadcrumbs
1 teaspoon cayenne
½ teaspoon black pepper

Directions

Preheat oven to 350 degrees. Lightly grease a large casserole baking dish with one tablespoon of the butter. Cook pasta according to package directions. Cook the sausage until it is browned and remove and drain on paper towels. Pour off but 1 tablespoon of fat from the pan. Add the onions, bell peppers and cook stirring for 3 minutes. Add the garlic and the anise seed and cook for 1 more minute. Remove from heat.

Melt the butter in a large, heavy saucepan over medium heat. Add the flour, stirring constantly with a wooden spoon, cook over medium heat until thick, being careful not to let the flour brown. Using a whisk, add the milk and cook, whisking constantly, until thick and smooth, about 5 minutes. Add the salt, cayenne and 2 cups of the cheese and stir well.

Add the noodles, cooked sausage and vegetables and stir well to combine. Pour into baking dish. In a mixing bowl, combine the remaining 1 cup of cheese with the breadcrumbs. Sprinkle over the macaroni and bake until golden brown about 25 minutes. Remove from oven and rest for 5 minutes before serving.

Scallops and Asparagus in Abby J's "Smokin' Hot" Sauce
Serves 4

Ingredients
1 lb. asparagus
1 tablespoon butter
1 tablespoon vegetable oil
2 teaspoons chopped garlic
4 scallions chopped
1 teaspoon grated fresh ginger
1 pound bay scallops
½ teaspoon kosher salt
1 small red chile finely chopped
3 tablespoons of *Abby J's Smokin Hot Sauce*
Lime Wedges

Directions
Trim the asparagus into 1-inch pieces and remove the tough edges. Heat the butter and oil in a skillet. Stir-fry the garlic, scallions, and ginger for one minute. Do not brown. Add the asparagus and scallops and continue stir-frying 4-5 minutes on high heat. Stir in the salt, lime zest, lime juice, chile, and smokin' hot sauce. Serve garnished with Lime wedges and freshly cooked basmati rice.

Sweet Bourbon Potatoes
Serves 6

Ingredients
6 sweet potatoes ½ inch thick
5 tablespoons unsalted butter
2 teaspoons cayenne pepper
¾ cup brown sugar
¾ cup Bourbon
3 tablespoons of sorghum syrup
Pinch of salt and pepper

Directions:
Preheat oven to 350 degrees.
Grease a casserole dish with 2 tablespoons of butter. Add the cayenne pepper along with the salt and pepper to the sweet potatoes and put into casserole dish. Melt the butter and then add sugar, bourbon, and sorghum syrup. Bring to a boil and then take off the heat and pour over the sweet potatoes. Bake for about 1 hour and turn sweet potatoes occasionally. This makes a great side dish for pork loin.

"Smokin' Hot" Baked Beans
Serves 8-10

Ingredients
2 ½ cups chopped onion
1 cup chicken broth
6 ounces chorizo, thinly sliced
¼ packed brown sugar
¼ cup vinegar
½ cup *Abby J's Smokin Hot Sauce*
¼ cup dark molasses
2 teaspoons dry mustard
2 teaspoons chipotle chile powder
¼ salt
¼ ground cloves

Smokin' Hot Baked Beans continued . . .

¼ ground allspice
1 (15 -ounce) can black beans, rinsed and drained
1 (15-ounce) can kidney beans, rinsed and drained
1 (15-ounce) can pinto beans, rinsed and drained

Directions:
Preheat oven to 325 degrees.
Heat a dutch oven oven medium-high heat. Add chorizo; sauté 2 minutes. Add onion; sauté 5 minutes, stirring occasionally. Stir in broth and remaining ingredients; bake uncovered at 325 for 1 hour.

Oven Fried Okra
Serves 4

Ingredients
1 lb.- 3 cups fresh okra, trimmed and cut ¾ inch
1 large egg
1 teaspoon cayenne pepper
½ cup fat-free buttermilk
1 ½ cup cornmeal
¾ teaspoon salt
½ teaspoon ground pepper
Cooking Spray

Directions
Preheat oven to 450 degrees.
Combine cornmeal, salt, black pepper, and red pepper in a dish and set aside. Combine buttermilk and egg in a large bowl, stirring with a whisk. Add the okra and toss to coat. Let stand 5 minutes. Dredge okra in cornmeal mixture. Place okra on pan coated with cooking spray. Bake for 35 to 40 minutes stirring occasionally. Sprinkle with salt.

Potato Salad
Serves 4-6

Ingredients
6 large red potatoes, peeled and cubed
1 medium Vidalia onion chopped
¾ cup celery chopped
4 hard-boiled eggs chopped
3 tablespoons of sweet pickle relish
¾ cup Duke's mayonnaise
2 tablespoons of jalapeño mustard
1 tablespoon cilantro, chopped
Paprika to garnish

Directions
Boil cubed potatoes until they are tender. Drain and cool. In a large bowl add celery, onion, eggs and pickle relish. Add mayonnaise, cilantro and mustard. Stir well and sprinkle with paprika and salt. Let the potato salad chill at least 3 hours or overnight before serving.

Mexican Grill Corn
Serves 4 to 6

Ingredients
4 ears corn, husk and silk removed, cut in half
2 tablespoons butter at room temperature
½ cup Parmesan cheese or Mexican blend cheese
3 tablespoons Duke's mayonnaise
½ teaspoon chili powder
1 lime cut into wedges

Directions
Heat grill to high. Place cheese in a bowl and set aside. Brush corn with butter and season with salt and pepper. Grill, turning every 2 to 3 minutes, until tender and slightly charred. This takes about 12 minutes. Let cool for 3 minutes. Brush corn with Duke's and roll in cheese to coat. Sprinkle with chili powder and serve with lime wedges.

Soup

Greek Soup

Ingredients
3 to 4 Springer Mountain Chicken Breast
2 lemons, squeezed
1 egg
1 cup of white rice

Directions
Boil chicken breasts for 20 minutes, making sure you use enough water to cover the chicken. Strain the chicken and pick the meat off the bone. Set aside. Put a cup of white rice into the chicken broth and cook until done. Do not boil too hard because you will boil your broth away. Beat the egg in the mixing bowl, adding the lemon juice slowly. You want the egg and lemon juice mix to be frothy.
Add the chicken broth slowly to the egg and lemon mixture and continue to beat. Turn the heat off of the broth and rice and add the lemon, egg and chicken broth back into the pan. This is a great recipe for a cold winter's day!

Taco Soup

Ingredients
1 pound lean ground beef
2 cans kernel corn
1 can pinto beans
1 can light red kidney beans
1 can black beans
1 28-ounce can diced tomatoes
1 jar *Abby J's Blackhawk Bean and Jalapeño Salsa*
1 onion, chopped
1 package ranch dressing mix
1 package taco seasoning mix
Optional: garlic powder, chili powder, salt and pepper (To taste)

Directions
Brown beef and onion. Mix all ingredients together.
Simmer for 30 minutes and then serve.

Jams & Jelly's

Abby J's Pepper Jelly
Makes 6 half pints

Ingredients
4 cups finely chopped green bell pepper
1 cup finely chopped jalapeño
1 ¼ cups cider vinegar
3 tablespoons pectin
2 cups sugar
1 cup honey
6- 8 oz. jelly jars

Directions
Prepare water canner. Heat jars in simmering water until ready for use. Do not boil. Wash lids in soapy water and set bands aside. Combine green bell peppers, jalapeños peppers and vinegar in a large saucepan. Gradually stir in pectin. Bring to a full rolling boil that cannot be stirred down over high heat, stirring constantly. Add sugar and honey. Return mixture to a full rolling boil. Boil for 3 minutes, stirring constantly. Remove from heat. Skim foam from top. Ladle hot jelly into hot jars, leaving ¼ head space. Wipe rim and center lid on jar. Screw band on tight. Process filled jars in a boiling water canner for 10 minutes. Remove jars and cool. Check seal after 24 hours. Lid should not flex up and down when center is pressed.

Raspberry Habanero Jam
Makes 5 1-pint

Ingredients
2 (12 ounces) packages frozen raspberries
1 ½ cups white vinegar
1 green pepper, halved and seeded
6 habanero peppers, stemmed
6 cups white sugar
3 tablespoons powdered pectin
5 1-pint canning jars

Directions
Blend vinegar, green bell pepper, and habanero peppers together in a blender until smooth. Stir pepper mixture, sugar, raspberries, and pectin powder in a large stockpot; bring to a boil and cook until jam is smooth and the sugar is dissolved, about 5 to 6 minutes. Sterilize the jars and lids in boiling water for at least 5 minutes. Pack jam into hot, sterilized jars, filling to ¼ inch of the top. Run a knife or thin spatula around the insides of the jars to remove any air bubbles. Wipe the rims of the jars with a moist paper towel to remove any food residue. Top with lids and screw on rings. I use a water canner and I fill this large canner halfway with water. Bring to a boil and lower jars into the boiling water using a holder. Leave a 2 inch space between the jars. Pour in more water if necessary to bring the water level to at least 1 in above the tops of the jars. Bring the water to a rolling boil, cover the pot and process for 15 minutes. Remove the jars from the stockpot and place onto a wood surface, several inches apart until cool. Once cool, press the top of each lid with a finger, ensuring proper seal and the lid does not move up or down. Store in cool area.

Bread

❧✦❧

When I break bread with friends and family it gives me great joy.

Cast Iron Blackhawk Corn Bread

Serves 6

Ingredients

2 cups cornmeal
1 ½ cups buttermilk
1 large egg beaten
4 tablespoons unsalted butter
1 ½ teaspoons kosher salt
½ teaspoons baking powder
½ teaspoon baking soda
1 jalapeño diced
2 ounces of bacon fat

Directions

Preheat oven for 450 degrees. Preheat large cast iron skillet with bacon fat for 15 minutes. While pan is preheating, combine the cornmeal, salt, baking powder and baking soda in a bowl. Whisk to combine ingredients. Combine remaining buttermilk, peppers and egg with a spatula. Pour the batter equally into the skillet. Place the skillet back in the oven for 10-12 minutes or until the bread has just set. It should be light golden brown. As soon as you take the bread out, put butter on top and spread evenly. Serve warm.

Abby J's Pumpkin Bread

Makes one loaf

Ingredients

4 eggs
4 cups sugar
3 ½ cups all purpose flour
2 cups pumpkin puree
1 cup oil
2 teaspoons baking soda
1 ½ teaspoon nutmeg
1 teaspoon cinnamon
1 teaspoon salt

½ teaspoon cloves
¼ teaspoon ginger

Directions

Preheat oven to 350 degrees. Grease and flour three 7 x 3 loaf pans. You can also make muffins or one large loaf with this recipe. In a large bowl, mix together pumpkin puree, eggs, oil, water and sugar until well blended. In a separate bowl, whisk together the flour, baking soda, salt, cinnamon, nutmeg, cloves and ginger. Stir the dry ingredients into the pumpkin mixture until just blended. Bake for 50 minutes in the preheated oven. Loaves are done when a toothpick inserted in the center comes out clean.

Zucchini Bread

Makes one loaf

Ingredients

2 eggs
1 cup sugar
1 cup fresh zucchini, shredded with skin
1 ½ cups all-purpose flour
½ cup vegetable oil
1 ½ teaspoons cinnamon
1 teaspoon vanilla
½ teaspoon baking soda
½ teaspoon salt
½ teaspoon nutmeg
½ teaspoon ginger
1/8 teaspoon baking powder
Zest of one lemon

Directions

Preheat oven to 325 degrees. In a large bowl, beat eggs and sugar until foamy. Add oil, zucchini and vanilla. Stir to blend. Combine flour, baking soda, salt, baking powder, lemon zest and spices. Add dry ingredients to zucchini mixture. Mix well. Pour into greased and floured loaf pan (9 x 5 inch). Bake for 1 hour at 325 degrees or until a wooden pick inserted in the center comes out clean.

Photo > Wade Collins

Abby J's Jalapeño Corn Muffins
Serves 6

Ingredients
1 cup buttermilk cornmeal
1 cup of milk
1 large egg
¾ cup sharp cheddar cheese
½ cup jalapeños
½ cup diced onions
½ cup cracklings optional
2 tablespoons light shortening
½ teaspoon baking soda
½ teaspoon salt

Directions
Preheat oven to 375 degrees and lightly grease an 8 x 8 muffin pan. Whisk together the cornmeal, baking soda and salt in a large mixing bowl. In a separate bowl, beat together the egg and milk. Make a well in the center of the dry ingredients and start adding the milk and egg. Add remaining ingredients and mix well. Pour mix in muffin pan, three-quarters full. Bake for 20 minutes or until golden brown. Serve hot.

Desserts

Blackhawk Cobbler
Serves 8

Cobbler Filling Ingredients
2 pounds of blackberries or mixed berries
Juice of one lemon
½ cup sugar plus 4 tablespoons
2 tablespoons cornstarch
1 teaspoon ground ginger
½ teaspoon ground cinnamon

Cobbler Topping Ingredients
2 ¼ cups all purpose flour
¾ cup heavy cream
½ cup packed brown sugar
¼ cup finely minced crystallized ginger
6 tablespoons unsalted butter, cut into pieces
1 large egg
2 teaspoons baking powder
1 teaspoon baking soda
1 teaspoon salt

Directions
Preheat oven to 375 degrees and lightly butter a 9 x13 inch baking dish. Combine the berries, lemon juice, ½ cup sugar, cornstarch, cinnamon and ground ginger. Toss to coat the berries evenly. Pour the berry mixture into the prepared baking dish. Stir the flour, brown sugar, baking powder, salt and baking soda. Add the butter, cutting it into the mixture until mix is coarse.

In a small bowl, whisk together the egg and cream. Slowly pour the egg mixture into the flour mixture, stirring until it holds together. Stir in the crystallized ginger. Using a spoon, place dollops of topping evenly over the berries, leaving a ¾-inch border uncovered. Sprinkle the 4 tablespoon of sugar over this mixture. Bake for 35 minutes or until golden brown. Take out, and let cool for 20 minutes. You can substitute apples or peaches in this recipe.

Fresh Bananas and Caramel
Serves 8

Ingredients
6 bananas, sliced
1 ¼ cups brown sugar firmly packed
¼ cup half and half
¼ cup butter
1 ½ teaspoon vanilla
¼ cups confection sugar
Sour cream

Directions
Mix brown sugar, half and half, and butter in a pot. Cook over low heat stirring constantly until it thickens. Remove from heat and add vanilla. Arrange sliced bananas in serving dish. Pour sauce over bananas and let cool. Mix sour cream and confection sugar well. Spoon over bananas and chill. This is especially attractive in parfait dishes. Serve same day as prepared.

Old Fashioned Pumpkin Pie
Serves 8

Ingredients
1 deep pie crust
2 cups farm fresh pumpkin puree
1 ½ cups heavy cream
¼ cup white sugar
2 eggs plus the yolk of a third egg
2 teaspoons ground cardamom
2 teaspoons ground cinnamon
1 teaspoon ground ginger
½ teaspoon salt
½ teaspoon lemon zest
¼ teaspoon ground nutmeg
¼ teaspoon ground cloves

Directions
Preheat oven to 425 degrees. Mix sugars, salt, spices and lemon zest in a large bowl. Beat the eggs and add them to the bowl. Stir in the pumpkin puree. Whisk all together until well incorporated. Pour into pie shell. Bake at 425 degrees for 15 minutes, then reduce heat to 350 degrees and bake for 40 to 50 minutes. Cool on a rack for 2 hours.

Bacon-Bourbon Brownies with Pecans
Makes 2 Dozen

Ingredients
½ pound sliced bacon
1 stick butter plus 2 tablespoons
4 eggs
1 ½ cups all-purpose flour
1 cup sugar
8 ounces bittersweet chocolate, chopped
2 ounces unsweetened chocolate, chopped
½ cup pecans
½ cup packed light brown sugar
¼ cup unsweetened cocoa powder
4 tablespoons bourbon
2 tablespoons bacon fat

Directions
Preheat oven 350 degrees and toast the pecans. Let cool and chop the nuts. In a skillet cook the bacon until crisp, about 6 minutes, and finely chop. In a saucepan, combine both chocolates with the butter and stir over very low heat until melted; transfer into a large bowl. Using a handheld mixer, beat in the sugar and light brown sugar with the bacon fat. Beat in the bourbon. Add the eggs and salt and beat until smooth. Sift the cocoa and flour into bowl until blended. Line a 9-inch square baking pan with parchment paper, allowing 2 inches of overhang on two opposite sides. Scrape the batter into the prepared pan and sprinkle the bacon bits and toasted pecans on top. Bake until brownies are set around the edges about 55 minutes. Take out of oven, and let the brownies cool completely. Lift the brownies out of the pan using the parchment paper. Cut brownies into squares.

Abby J's Sour Cream Lemon Pound Cake

Serves 12

Ingredients

3 ¼ cups all-purpose flour
2 ½ cups sugar
1 (8 ounce) carton low-fat sour cream
3 large eggs
1 cup powdered sugar
¾ cup butter, softened
¼ cup fresh lemon juice, divided
4 tablespoons dry graham cracker crumbs
1 ½ tablespoons grated lemon rind
2 teaspoons lemon extract
½ teaspoon baking soda
¼ teaspoon salt
Light cooking spray

Directions

Preheat oven to 350 degrees. Coat a 10-inch tube pan with cooking spray and dust with graham cracker crumbs. Combine flour, baking soda and salt in a bowl, stir well with a whisk.

Beat butter in a large bowl with a mixer at medium speed until light and fluffy. Add sugar and lemon extract, beating until well blended. Add the eggs one at a time, beating well after each addition. Add rind and 2 tablespoons lemon juice, and beat for 30 seconds. Add flour mixture to wet ingredients alternately with sour cream, beating at low speed, ending with flour mixture. Spoon mix into the prepared pan. Bake at 350 degrees for 1 hour and 10 minutes or until a toothpick inserted in center of cake comes out clean. Cool cake in pan for 15 minutes on a wire rack, and remove from pan. Allow cake to cool completely. Combine 2 tablespoons lemon juice and powdered sugar. Drizzle glaze over the top of cake and serve with fresh fruit and whipped cream.

Abby J's
Sour Cream
Lemon Pound Cake

Chocolate Fudge Cake

Serves 12

Ingredients

2 cups sugar
2 cups all purpose flour
1 stick butter
2 eggs
1 cup water
½ cup oil
½ cup buttermilk
3 ½ tablespoons cocoa
1 teaspoon baking soda
1 teaspoon pure vanilla extract

Directions

Preheat oven to 325 degrees. In a large mixing bowl, combine the sugar and flour.

In a medium saucepan, heat the butter, cocoa, water and oil until butter is melted. Pour over flour mixture and combine. Add the eggs, buttermilk, baking soda and vanilla, mixing well.

Pour batter into an ungreased 9 x 13-inch baking pan. Bake 40 minutes or until a toothpick inserted in the center of the cake comes out clean.

Fudge Icing

1 stick butter
¼ cup milk
3 ½ tablespoons cocoa powder
1 box confectioner's sugar
1 cup chopped pecans (optional)

Directions

In a medium saucepan, heat butter, milk and cocoa over medium heat until butter is melted.

Add pecans and pour over the hot cake.

Blueberry Coffee Cake

Serves 12

Ingredients

2 cups of fresh blueberries
2 cups all-purpose flour
¾ cup sugar
¾ cup buttermilk
½ cup vanilla yogurt
¼ cup butter, melted
2 ½ teaspoons baking powder
1 egg

Directions

Preheat oven to 350 degrees. In mixing bowl combine all ingredients except blueberries. Mix to blend. Carefully fold in blueberries. Pour mix into bundt pan. Sprinkle with crumble topping. Bake for 45 to 50 minutes.

Crumble Topping

Makes 1 ¼ cups
¾ cup all-purpose flour
½ cup sugar, packed
½ cup cold butter
½ teaspoon cinnamon

Directions

In a small bowl combine flour, sugar and cinnamon. Cut butter into mixture and sprinkle over cake.

Fruit Cake Cookies
Makes 5 Dozen

Ingredients
1 cup butter
1 ½ cups sugar
2 ½ cups all-purpose flour
2 eggs
½ teaspoon salt
½ teaspoon baking soda
1 ½ teaspoon cinnamon
1 ½ teaspoon vanilla
1 8 ounces candied pineapple
1 8 ounces candied cherries
1 8 ounces dates
2 cups pecans chopped

Preheat oven to 350 degrees. Prepare fruit and nuts by quartering pineapples, cherries, nuts and dates about the same size.
In a small bowl combine flour, salt, baking soda and cinnamon; set aside.
In a large mixing bowl, cream butter and sugar until fluffy. Add eggs and beat well. Add flour mixture and incorporate ingredients.
Stir in vanilla, fruits, and nuts. Place spoonfuls of dough onto cookie sheets and bake 12 minutes or until golden brown.
After cooling on cookie sheet for minutes transfer to wire rack.

Cocktails

Abby J's Jalapeño Margaritas
Makes 1 drink

Ingredients
3 cups tequila
1 ½ cups fresh lime juice
1 cup Grand Marnier
1 cup simple syrup
½ jalapeño pepper, sliced
lime and Jalapeño slices for garnish
Ice

Directions
Make jalapeño infused tequila: Add the jalapeños to the tequila, and let it sit at room temperature for a few hours. Remove jalapeños and pour infused tequila into a small serving glasses. Serve on the side so guests can add as much or little spice as they like. Mix the lime juice, Grand Marnier and simple syrup together. Add the spicy tequila to finish margaritas.

Farm Mint Mojitos
Makes 1 drink

Ingredients
1 ½ ounces white rum
10 fresh mint leaves
1 cup ice cubes
½ cup club soda
½ lime, cut into four wedges
2 tablespoons white sugar

Farm Mint Mojitos continued . . .

Directions
Place mint leaves and one lime wedge into a sturdy glass. Use muddler to crush the mint and release the mint oils and lime juice.
Add two more lime wedges and the sugar, and muddle again to release the lime juice. Fill the glass almost to the top with ice. Pour the rum over the ice, and fill the glass with club soda. Stir, taste and add more sugar if desired. Garnish with remaining lime wedge.

Jalapeño Martini
Makes 4 drinks

Ingredients
12 ounces vodka
1 large jalapeño, thinly sliced
3 tablespoons jalapeño pepper jelly

Directions
Chill four martini glasses. Mix together the vodka and pepper jelly, and shake in a martini shaker. Pour mix into the chilled glasses and garnish with the jalapeño slices.

Abby J's Jalapeño Martini

Limoncello

Makes 1 drink

Ingredients

1 liter vodka
8 lemons
2 tangerines
4 cups water
3 cups sugar

Directions

Zest the lemons and tangerines into a Ball Mason jar. Pour in the vodka. Cover, and let infuse for two weeks at room temperature in a dark place. After two weeks, combine sugar and water in a medium saucepan. Bring to a boil and continue stirring until sugar dissolves. Remove from heat and let cool for 10 to 15 minutes. Strain the vodka through a wire mesh strainer into the sugar and water mixture and discard the rinds. Cool completely and put mixture back into Mason jar and store in freezer. Can be stored in freezer up to one year.

Blackhawk Cape Codder

Makes 1 drink

Ingredients

3 ounces vodka
4 ounces cranberry juice
½ ounce fresh lime juice
Lime Wedge

Shake the liquid ingredients vigorously with ice. Strain into an ice-filled highball glass. Squeeze the lime wedge over the drink, and drop it in.

Chocolate Martini

Makes 1 drink

Ingredients

1 ½ ounces vodka
½ oz. Godiva chocolate liqueur
¼ oz. white creme de cacao
Bittersweet chocolate shavings

Shake the liquid ingredients vigorously with ice. Strain into a chilled cocktail glass and sprinkle with bittersweet chocolate shavings on top.

Lemon Drop Martini

Makes 1 drink

Ingredients

1 ½ oz. lemon flavored vodka
1 oz. Grand Marnier
1 ½ oz. fresh lemon juice
1/2 oz. fresh orange juice
Superfine sugar
Lemon wedge
Lemon peel spiral

Rub th rim of a chilled cocktail glass with the lemon wedge and rim with sugar. Shake the ingredients vigorously, with ice. Strain into the prepared glass. Garnish with the lemon peel spiral.

French Martini

Makes 1 drink

Ingredients

2 ounces vodka
½ ounce Chambord
1 ounce pineapple juice
Lemon twist

Shake the liquid ingredients vigorously with ice. Stain into a chilled cocktail glass. Twist the lemon peel over the drink, and drop it in. Enjoy on a hot summer afternoon.

Index

Continued on next page ..

Field Note

In the heart of the Southern Appalachian Mountains, a sauce is born. Hungry fishermen who spend the day angling for trophy trout on the picturesque Soque River conclude their day at Abby J's river house, looking for nourishment. The thrill of catching a 30-inch brown trout is enough to satisfy even the most experienced fisherman to ever toss a line, but when you visit Blackhawk, the fishing is only the beginning.

After landing several trophy brown and rainbow trouts, including the largest trout of my life on a barbless hook, I had worked up a huge appetite. Abby J brought me and my camera crew into her river house and fed us some chili. She said, "This is what I feed all of my fishermen", and I instantly realized yet another reason why people keep returning to Blackhawk. The chili was the best I'd ever had! My television story instantly shifted focus. A fish-tale for the ages was just trumped by a bowl of Abby J's chili. The entire crew had fun on the river, but we truly exhausted ourselves with seconds and thirds on the chili.

Some time later, I received an email from Abby J, letting me know that she had since begun a brand of salsas, and I was thrilled. All natural, locally grown and a perfect blend, so similar to that first dose of chili she fed me back in 2010. So … I decided to write this for my friend, the talented Abby J, and I sincerely hope a complimentary jar of her black bean and herb salsa, my favorite, is coming my way soon!

See you soon, Abby!

David Zelski
Host
Anglers & Appetites on Fox Sports South
Sun Sports Florida
Georgia Traveler / Georgia Public Broadcast System

Dream big!

Just when the caterpillar thought the world was ending… she turned into a butterfly.

*Thank you for joining me
on this journey!*

Kick back . . . and enjoy life !